CHANGING LANES
YOUR DREAMS ARE CLOSER THAN THEY APPEAR

ACKNOWLEDGMENTS:

This book is inspired by the people who have had a direct impact in my life, and those who have inspired me without knowing the impact you've made.

The motivation I get from my mom drives me to be a better person. Her unconditional love and praise encourages me to serve others. As a breast cancer conqueror, she has given hope to women around the world and changed the lives of so many. She has the cherubic ability to bring people to their faith, to keep fighting and to help people turn to God for guidance and strength.

My father is what every man should strive to become. He has led a life epitomized by success in everything he's set out to accomplish. Most importantly, he is the ultimate husband to my mom and a model father. His spiritual leadership has shaped my faith journey, and I will forever be grateful for his guidance along the way.

Brett and Ryan - you are the best brothers anyone could ask for. You've pushed me to pursue greatness in the important areas of life. Whenever I needed anything you've been there with open arms and hearts. I am proud of each of your unique gifts. You make life so much fun. More than just brothers, you're truly friends.

Melanie and Katie - you are the best sisters-in-law anyone could ask for. You married into our family, and by doing so, have made it more complete. The desire to support me in everything is greatly appreciated, and knowing we would do anything for each other means the world to me. You've become the sisters I never had.

This book is for each of you who have ever wanted more; for those who know you are a special gift made in the image and likeness of your Creator. But more, for those who have yet to discover how special and how valuable you are in this world. You inspire me to Change Lanes in my own life to build a lasting legacy.

Foreword

By: Greg S. Reid

Best Selling author of the Think and Grow Rich Series:

Three Feet From Gold, Stickabilty, and Thoughts Are Things.

Meeting Lane Ethridge in 2009 was one of those experiences you don't soon forget. It was a warm Tuesday evening when I entered the room and saw him on stage educating and empowering the attendees.

The first thing I noticed was that he was holding a beat up yardstick.

When I asked the VP of the company what he was using it for, he replied that he had it with him for the past 312 days everywhere he went.

When he finished his presentation, I asked him about the lengthy wood piece, and he proceeded to tell me that he had read a book that completely changed his life.

That book was "Three Feet From Gold," (represented by the three foot yardstick) co-authored with Sharon Lechter.

He claimed he had read the book at the perfect time in his life, and it had a dramatically powerful impact on him that inspired him to not give up before the miracle happened.

He carried the slim piece of wood to remind him to stay the course.

He attributes this journey as a defining Lane Change, that moment when things shift one way or another that dramatically impact our direction.

Lane and I instantly became friends.

Eventually, we co-authored the national bestselling book "Initiative" together as he truly represented the message.

My hope for you is that this book finds you at the perfect time in your life.

Take the counsel from "Changing Lanes" and not only read it, but adopt it as a part of your life.

When life hands us a detour, it could just be God's way of showing us a better direction.

Greg S. Reid

INTRODUCTION

I remember the frustrating times cleaning paper plates so that I could reuse them. I remember getting dinner at the same place I got gasoline for my car. I can still smell the coins laying on my apartment floor that I had to count to purchase the bare necessities. I was flat out broke and it flat out wasn't fun.

I was one month away from proposing to my girlfriend when I got a phone call from her letting me know she was moving on. When I opened the door that night to our apartment everything was gone. I felt as empty on the inside as a person as the inside of that vacant apartment.

I let her take our car, and now I was riding around on a bike in a new city with no real friends, no real connections, no real direction and really no idea what was going to happen in my life.

Soon after, my grandmother passed away.

Drinking every night to avoid my true feelings, I found myself going down a path that would eventually lead to a reality I wasn't happy with. One morning I woke up not knowing how I had gotten home.

Eventually I got a used car but it was repossessed.

The IRS put a levy on my bank accounts and I had no access to the little money I had.

I was alive, but I certainly wasn't living.

Then I discovered something that changed it all.

I went from walking through life blindly, to having a vision of where I wanted my life to be.

It gave me Purpose... Passion... Prosperity, and gave me the opportunity to impact people's lives in a way that made me feel truly alive.

The journey has lead me to meet some of the most amazing people, work with my family, build relationships that will last a lifetime, join forces with powerful individuals to change the world and, most importantly, have a purposeful intention to create a legacy.

You see, I had someone who cared enough about me give me an opportunity to make a change in my life, and I am giving you that same opportunity.

The only reason I am where I am today is because of a Lane Change, a turning point where I went in a new direction. I decided to take action. I yearned to be able to learn from those who had what I wanted, and I DIDN'T GIVE UP!

We have helped thousands of people get similar results in their life, and we want to help YOU.

The biggest mistake I see is people being closed minded and overly skeptical. And I get it. When I first thought about making a Lane Change I couldn't see past my current situation. So let me be up front with you that the journey will have its ups and downs and will be challenging. But so is living a small life.

Taking the next step allowed me to turn my dreams into reality. It helped me create a luxury lifestyle and have the time, freedom and the opportunities to do what I love.

This isn't about me though. It's about you.

My time is precious and so is yours.

If you don't want to take action and do what is needed to get what you want, then simply give this book to someone who wants a better life. But, if you want a big life for yourself, simply take the initiative and let's create your future together. It's time to make a shift and take your life into overdrive. It's time to put the pedal to the metal and get you in the fast lane to your best life. It's time for a Lane Change.

PART ONE

What Lane Are You In?

Have you ever had any challenges in life? Of course you have.

Have you ever been frustrated with not having enough money to do what you love? You're not alone.

Do you not have enough time to enjoy the life you want with those you love? Well, it's time you did.

The lane you are currently in is controlling your life.

"Let's face it. Breakthrough is NOT easy, and it's uncomfortable. You will have to break patterns, overcome adversity, and force yourself to do some things that are inconvenient and require some effort. The road to mediocrity is easy, that's why so many people continue to drive on it." – Ron Pagliarulo

We've all heard the supposed benefits of the old adage 'The power of positive thinking', but have you ever thought about what that really means? As humans, we are prone to predictive routines, mundane schedules and getting stuck in the ensuing ruts that lead to aggravation, and sometimes we even begin to feel completely deflated. We are left scratching our heads wondering if this is really what life is meant to be for us. By nature, it's the very definition of insanity—doing the same things over and over and expecting a different result. Our lives are a direct result of the choices we have made, plain and simple. It's time to take back control of your life – STOP the blame game and START a Lane Change.

We are either growing or we are retreating. Either way, we are changing every day of our lives. The reality is that if you do things the way you are now, you will have the same results. And with how fast times are changing, if you're not willing to grow, you will end up even further behind.

Our culture is changing, our environment is changing, technology is changing, politics are changing, the economy is changing and our health is changing. The question is, what are we going to do and how are we changing as a result.

There are some universal principles that permeate the lives of those achieving greatness. Leaders who are having success are all willing to adapt and change.

Yet, certain things that work in one circumstance won't be as effective in another. Need proof? We all learned that if we catch on fire we should 'Stop, drop and roll.' But how effective would that be if you were burning in hell? Probably not very.

Yet we continue to do ineffective things in our own lives wondering why we have ineffective results.

Some people try to use old school techniques to achieve results in a new world. The perspective on life that has led you to the life you are living currently is based upon your experiences, beliefs and those people you choose to surround yourself with. It will require a completely different paradigm shift to create a life you design. It will take a powerful Lane Change to set you on the road to your best life.

There have been several studies conducted over the years that have shown Americans would rather die than change—Yes, you read that correctly. Change is the most difficult process people undergo, and they often resist it with every fiber of their being. It brings with it a level of self-introspection that most would rather avoid at all costs. Change means a loss of control, numerous uncertainties, unwelcome surprises, hard work, and stepping outside of one's comfort zone. For most, the fear of the unknown is overwhelming and paralyzes any opportunity for growth, and this is why so many of us are stuck in the same place day after day, month after month and year after year. But I promise you this, IT DOESN'T HAVE TO BE THAT WAY!

I was just like many people a few years ago. Lost, in a job I had no passion for, freshly un-coupled, and longing for something more. I decided to Change Lanes—permanently. It was the toughest, yet most rewarding choice I've ever made and I'm here to help you take that same journey towards true happiness and financial freedom. Changing Lanes is the first step in fulfilling your dreams, ultimately leading you down the path of true success.

How Did You Get In That Lane?

"When obstacles occur, change your path, not your destination." –Doug Crowe

There comes a point in everyone's life when he or she has to take a serious look in the mirror and realize that everything in life is a choice. If we want to change, we need a reprogramming of our mindset.

Our lives are merely a reflection of the choices we make.

You're the only one who can and must assume responsibility for yourself, and you're the only one who can clarify what your real priorities are for your life. This begins by determining what's important to you. The choices you make control your priorities and, as a result, your lifestyle. Your choices are far more powerful than your circumstances, and you have the power to enhance your life by making better choices.

Now, don't hear what I'm not saying. I am not saying other people are not important. I am not saying that the things that happen to us don't affect us. I am not saying that you should be selfish.

What I am merely suggesting is too often we cast everything on anything but our own decisions. We deflect personal responsibility and aren't willing to take personal accountability. Why? Because it's so much easier to blame others for our lives than own up to our own egos.

What choices are you making in your life, and are you willing to confirm those choices have created your current situation?

The choices we make determine the outcomes that those choices create.

When life is going well, you make particular choices. When life is not going as well, it may cause you to make different choices.

But at the end of the day, life is simply a series of choices.

We need to understand that it's all about making choices and then sticking to those decisions, no matter how many influences we have, how many unfortunate circumstances happen to us or the people in our lives and their influence on us.

The first and most important step to changing lanes is understanding how you ended up where you are in the first place. This step is often skipped in the mad rush to the finish line, which only leads to roadblocks and more speed bumps. Growth cannot take place without fully grasping the 'why's' of your current situation. Otherwise, change will be temporary and more frustrating than sitting in construction traffic.

"Success lies within each of us regardless of our background or our experiences. All success is the compounding effects of our thoughts and actions towards a definite goal." - Aldo Vides

The Vides family migrated from El Salvador in order to give their children a better life and the opportunities that only the United States could offer. They worked multiple jobs in order to provide for their family, and struggled for many years. But it was all worth it when their youngest son, Aldo, graduated from San Diego State University in 2010.

But all was not well in Aldo's life.

Aldo began drinking heavily during college and became quite the partier. This lifestyle followed him after graduation with devastating consequences. Later that year, after a night of drinking, he was pulled over and arrested for DUI. His family was devastated, and he had disappointed not only them, but himself. This was the lowest point of his life, and he had no idea how he could have such a promising future one minute, and be in a jail cell the next. His life, as he knew it, was over. And it would take him 2 long years to fully recover.

The arrest and ensuing court appearance shook Aldo to the core. He knew he had to make a major shift—a Lane Change—before it was too late.

He had always been drawn to personal development books, such as "Think and Grow Rich" and "The Secret", but had stopped short of implementing their messages. Aldo realized the time had come to incorporate the wisdom of these books; he committed to re-read them, and read several more that would shape his beliefs.

While simultaneously working a full time corporate job, he began absorbing everything he could get his hands on in regards to self-actualization and personal development.

He went from consuming alcohol to consuming the knowledge and wisdom from those who had what he wanted. In doing this, he realized it was time to pursue his new-found desires.

Soon he discovered his passion for real estate. He also understood the importance of surrounding himself with people who could teach and guide him along this path, and started working with mentors that he met through Secret Knock, CEO Space, and FortuneBuilders. He partnered up with a local investor and spent 2 years learning the real estate business— corporate job by day and real estate by night.

He discovered that the more he learned, the more he wanted to know. This insatiable appetite for knowledge led to Aldo quitting his "real job" and taking on his dream full time. At 28 years old, Aldo now heads up a real estate investing firm and has his life back on track.

Aldo understood what it was like to have parents who worked two jobs to help their family. He didn't want to do the same thing, and discovered that he had an opportunity to create a life where he was in control. Moreover, he wanted to give back to his parents for supporting him when he needed them the most.

One of the things that Aldo always emphasizes is the love and support of his family. Without them, he never would have been able to turn his life around. He feels he owes his current successes to their sacrifice and refusal to give up on him when so many others did.

More importantly than the money that comes from his passion is the personal growth that comes from the journey. He shifted gears and took control of his life and his future. There were nights that Aldo literally couldn't remember, but is constantly reminded how important life is and how precious his relationships are to him. He is giving back to the community and making an impact in the world. He understands that he has become a mentor to others and needs to lead by example. Continually improving, Aldo takes the wisdom and counsel of one of his mentors, Than Merrill, who told him, "What you do today is how you will be remembered tomorrow."

You can't change your life in a day but your life can certainly change in a moment. Sometimes we need to change the direction we are headed in order to create a new reality and a better future.

Aldo was given a second chance in life and he doesn't take that lightly. He has transformed his mind and his body and is beyond dedicated to those most important in his life. He has taken his purpose and passion into overdrive and the road ahead is wide open!

Without vision, there is no future. How can you possibly get somewhere if you have no idea where you're going? Vision is your GPS on the road of life— it keeps you headed in the right direction.

The road to success is paved with many who have started and stopped, only to give up when the journey proved tough. Those are the types who are wandering around aimlessly hoping to run into happiness one day without putting in any efforts of their own. They go right back to who they've always been because they never took the time to find out how they got there to begin with. These are the sorts that will try to stomp all over your dreams in an effort to ease the pain of their own disappointments. Avoid these people at all costs! Negative people DO NOT inspire positive change—only positive people can do that.

Growing up in Maryland, our summers were filled with summer vacations at the beach and enjoying crab feasts with friends and family that would last the entire day. The smell of Old Bay would circle the air and the sound of cracking shells would evoke a sense of freedom, peace and serenity. Surrounded by the white sand and the white-capped

Atlantic Ocean, life was a breeze. Crabs were a part of our culture and also became a part of the way my view on life came to be. You see, when crabs are caught they are tossed in a bushel to be cooked. All of the crabs have been taken out of their natural environment and have been cast into a new reality by someone else's power over them. Fighting for their lives, they attempt to climb out of the bushel to freedom. As one begins to near the top rim of the bushel, the other crabs pull it back into the group and the struggle to escape continues.

Often we surround ourselves with people who will do the same. We want to escape from our circumstances and chase freedom. The desire to go after our dreams and pursue a life worth living is challenged by those who want to pull us down. They are crabby and because of their desire to settle and live a simple life they feel the need to have you join them. But you're greater than that. You're a Lane Changer. You need to take a mallet to your limiting beliefs and crack open a life of passion, purpose and create a life so unbelievable that people will wonder how you achieved so much. At first they will laugh at you and to pull you down. Then they will want your help in pulling them out of their circumstances. Escape a life of mediocrity and enter a life of exceptional. Changing Lanes is about helping yourself and becoming someone so fulfilled that you cannot help but change the lives of those around you.

I'm willing to take this journey with you, but I need your unwavering commitment to do what it takes to be a Lane Changer, not only for yourself, but for others too. Ask yourself these questions: What does your current lane say about you? Why are you toiling away in the slow lane? How did you even get on that particular road? Have you veered off into a ditch somewhere along the way? Are you tired of looking in the rear view mirror? And most importantly, are you finally ready to Change Lanes?

The human race is by nature selfish and lazy. It takes work to put the greater good ahead of our own personal interests and to put in the time and effort necessary to achieve success. As we all know, if it was easy, everyone would be doing it.

You must have confidence in your decisions, and see them through. Being wishy-washy will only cloud your judgment and prevent those around you from seeing you as a leader. Remember, it's only a mistake if you don't learn anything from it.

Life is merely a reflection of the decisions we make and the actions we take, which lead us to our current reality, ultimately determining our final destination.

Every experience and relationship in our lives is a stepping stone that leads us toward the designed life we deserve.

Are you living a life you are proud of? Great, you've made great choices OR you've learned from the poor choices you've made and made a Lane Change.

Are you living a life in which you feel you are not living up to your purpose?

It's simply time to reflect on why that is and determine the course corrections necessary to get where you envision your life.

The beauty of it all? You get to decide how you want your life to unfold. A quote from one of my favorite books encourages us that if you "Ask you shall receive; seek and you shall find; knock and the door will be opened." We have the freedom to create. So what do you want your life to look like? Who are the people in your life and should they be allowed in your life? What are the things in your life and why do you possess them? What characteristics do you possess and who shaped you to believe how you view yourself?

You should also take pride in knowing that you were designed by the image and likeness of God. He created you specifically to be a part of this world and your gifts, talents and treasures are unique, which makes you unique and means you are not supposed to be anyone else. You can certainly aspire to be like someone you respect. We have the freedom to learn from those who have placed in our lives to guide us. However, it is paramount that we follow counsel – wisdom, knowledge and expertise from people who have been where we want to go. The crabs and dream stealers live their lives based on opinion – lack of knowledge, inexperience and a life they created based upon their fear and driven by scarcity.

It's time you take to heart your uniqueness, your power and how much you are loved. And rejoice in your greatness!!

Once you understand you have been given permission to pursue your purpose and dreams with passion, and you delight in the gift of life, you will not want to live any other way.

If there was ever a time to follow your passion and do something that matters to you, that time is most certainly now.

How Committed are You to Your Lane?

Make a decision.

Often times it's easy and obvious. Other times it's challenging and discouraging.

There comes a time where you realize that if you're not where you want to go, it's time for a Lane Change.

Indecision is a form of paralysis and is in and of itself, a decision. Nothing great was ever accomplished by indecision. You cannot let fear be your guide, but instead use it to fuel your courage and sense of purpose. Ignorance on fire will always get you further than knowledge on ice. But when you have knowledge on fire you will create a path to success that will lead you to everything you desire.

So many of us believe we have to sacrifice ourselves, and our happiness, to save others. THIS IS A MYTH! The best thing we can do for those we love is to take care of ourselves—mentally, physically and spiritually. Doggedly holding onto ideals and thought processes that are not working and never will is NOT the path to success.

I'm living proof that changing lanes is key to becoming who you are meant to be. I'll try anything once, but if it's not working, I change tactics, no matter how uncomfortable. That does not mean that I give up on my goals. It just means that I may need to change the methods to be able to achieve them. I'm a true believer that God will continue to give us the same lessons until we learn what we are supposed to learn. And as humans, we can be terribly stubborn and tend to get in our own way. It's time to take a good, hard look in the mirror and decide what you want more: success or comfort. If you choose success, keep reading. If you're going to go with comfort, there's no need to finish this book— nobody can help you if you won't help yourself.

The reality is you are not where you want to be or you wouldn't be this far into this book.

And even more of reality is that you probably won't be where you want to be a few years from now either. Why? Because most people are too focused not on where they are going but where they are coming from. They are being pushed around; pushed by what others want for them more than what they want for themselves. We are either running from our fears or running to our dreams. Too often, the thoughts that permeate our mind are how to escape where we currently are and we never focus on where we want to go. But the mind doesn't care about what you want it cares about what you think about.

The rearview mirror is smaller than the windshield merely so that you can look back to see how far you've come, but you should focus on where you are going!

"Let your life be led by your soul." – Joe Zanotelli

As the youngest of 5 children, Joe was often singled out by his siblings and received the brunt of their teasing and taunting. This typical sibling interaction, combined with his birth order, created a lifetime of insecurities. He was continuously feeling as though he was living someone else's life. Joe became easily manipulated due to his need to feel accepted by his older brothers and sisters, and this set the precedent for the rest of his life. While his parents have been married over 50 years and fostered a healthy environment for their children, Joe felt like he wasn't ever part of his own family.

Throughout the formative years of childhood, Joe never developed a sense of who he was. His environment at home didn't give him the ability to become a leader or to have his voice heard. He became a follower feeling isolated and ostracized by everyone around him. His first relationship when he was entering college brought him to find companionship, temporarily.

Unfortunately, she cheated on him, which destroyed their relationship and what little confidence Joe had in himself.

He struggled with the decision in telling his mother, fearing how it would affect her. And his fears were well founded. She broke down crying and was deeply hurt by what had taken place. This led Joe to feel as if he couldn't share with her anymore because it hurt her too much. Now he was left completely alone in the world, with no one to help shoulder the burdens of life.

Two years later, he fell in love with the woman who would eventually become his wife of 22 years. She exposed him to the wonders of the world and helped him see there was so much more than these 4 walls, but the same feelings from childhood plagued him still. He believed yet again, he was living someone else's life. He had traded the life his parents and siblings wanted him to live, for the life his wife wanted to live. Even though Joe knew this intrinsically, he couldn't get to the point of actually giving it up. And then disaster struck once again.

Seven years into the marriage, his wife had an affair. This reaffirmed his fear of being alone and he was thrust into a period of loneliness and isolation, with no one to turn to for help or guidance. Through counseling they were able to keep the marriage together, however, the trust with his wife would never be mended. They continued to travel and had distractions, including a condo in downtown San Diego where they partied, thus becoming a replacement for the real life he wanted to live. They were living the big life, but an empty life. He wasn't able to shift out of the relationship. This led to an even bigger disconnect, yet all Joe craved was a connection to someone or something.

Adding to the pressures weighing heavily on the marriage, Joe and his wife had been unable to conceive. Years of doctors and fertility treatments resulted in an even deeper divide between the two. Eventually

they adopted a daughter and son. Joe
felt he finally had the connection and
meaning in his life he had always
sought. But because his thought
patterns remained the same, the
children just became another avenue in
his life that someone else controlled,
namely his wife.

Joe's wife continued to make all the
decisions, both for the marriage and
for the kids. She was still in authority
over him as she always had been and
he began to feel as if he was being
nudged out of his kid's lives. This was

the catalyst in Joe's life – his Lane Change.

He found himself soul searching and asking, "What am I doing?" Through a life of denial he was led down a road that was defined by someone else's wants, needs and desires. At this moment Joe made the decision that he wasn't going to take a backseat to his own life any longer. Joe finally gave himself permission to think and do for himself. He discovered that he has to have the belief that he is bigger than himself. Once he could do that, he could be who he was truly meant to be.

An answered prayer came in the form of a physical book that literally showed up on his doorstep. To this day he still doesn't know how it arrived at his home. This book helped him believe that he was deserving of blessings, his own and not just someone else's. He believed he was worthy of owning his own life and molding it according to his own desires. Changing Lanes wasn't an option, it was a conviction for Joe.

From that inspiration, Joe realized that

he could never complete his Lane Change while still in his troubled marriage. He had to make the difficult decision to seek divorce.

Once he forged ahead, Joe began to have faith in himself and in the people who were being brought into his life during this critical time. He had faith in the books and personal development material that manifested itself at the right time when he needed it the most.

Joe confidently believes that his intention leads to his beliefs and the actions behind those are what is creating his new reality. He has the power to look back long enough to see what he wasn't satisfied with and now possesses the strength to look forward to what possibilities are coming his way.

One of the intentions Joe had was to rekindle his relationship with his family. He wanted that connection with them that he didn't have growing up. He wasn't sure how they would react and or if they would be open to repairing the dysfunction after all this time. But he took action. He picked up the phone and called them, expressing his intent. Joe had a deep-rooted belief that they would accept his desire and he stood in his power and his core beliefs. He was unwavering in his commitment to his intent and the shift into the belief that it would cultivate a life he envisioned.

After reconnecting with his family, Joe felt the need to give back to his community. He stepped up to be the executive director for a non-profit helping inner city kids achieve academic success and follow their dreams of getting into college. More importantly, he pours into their lives and provides the encouragement and companionship he didn't receive growing up. Joe has become a reputed big brother to many as he continues to grow the organization in hopes of helping kids for years to come.

Joe's dedication to his vision has allowed him to step into his power in other areas of his life. He has discovered that his passion for engineering has faded and his passion for people has grown. He is now engineering a life of purpose, pursuing his ultimate life. And the best part is, Joe is helping others mold their greatness as well. His Lane Change has led others to create their own Lane Changes. His gift of helping others uncover their intent and beliefs has fueled a whole new perspective. It's almost as if Joe has given birth to his own inner child – living the life he dreamed of rather than the one others wanted for him.

We all face the proverbial fork in the

road. The question isn't which road will you take. The question is, will you take the road of intent, guided by your soul, believing with all of your being that it will lead to a life YOU desire?

Our lives are a series of stepping stones. When I was a middle school teacher I read a book that altered the way I looked at life and transformed my path. It launched my life of a commitment to personal development and becoming the person I am today and continue to become as I change lanes along my journey. That led me to become a real estate investor and by flipping houses successfully I began to have a desire to teach again. Yet, I had the freedom to teach those who desired to learn from me rather than simply educating teenagers because they were moving through the public education system and forced to be in my classroom. The passion for helping others led me to teaching others how to create success. That led me to building an International business helping others build their own businesses. That opportunity led me to public speaking which allowed me to co-author a National Bestselling book with some of the foremost experts in personal development. Ultimately, those experiences and wisdom led me to writing this book to empower YOU to be a visionary for your life and the lives for millions around the world.

You are a Lane Changer and it's time to build your legacy.

So, are you ready? Do you have the stones?

This is the time to adopt into your life the actions you are going to take for yourself. You will be able to create a vision for yourself so strong that you will no longer be pushed by your reality but pulled by your vision.

We are all motivated by our fears or by our dreams. Remember, most of us are too afraid to fully chase our dreams, because we may actually catch them. You need to determine if you are motivated by the carrot or the stick. Do you accomplish more when you are punished for not achieving what you want or do you accomplish more by the reward of that achievement? You are either a carrot or stick person. But let's take that one step further. What can you do to make this more real?

Make a Dream Board – a visual representation of what you want in your life. Then make a Fear Board – a visual representation of what would be a life you would never want (for some you may be there now)!

Put them side by side. Which one evokes more emotions?

If you don't do what you need will those fears remain in your life? If you do what you need will you get closer to those things on your Dream Board?

One of my favorite books says, "Without vision, the people will perish." And some of you are perishing right now because you don't have a vision strong enough to allow you to truly live!

Once you know why you are driven, it's time to realize it has nothing to do with you, yet it has everything to do with you. Most of us are living on an unconscious level that controls your life without you being aware. We're robots in a human body. As soon as you can get control of your thoughts you can consciously create your life.

And when you know how to control your thoughts you have a better chance of controlling your choices. When you control your choices you take personal responsibility. And when you take personal responsibility you have the ability to live a life that affords you the opportunity to serve others because you are not living inwardly focused.

When I first saw the 'M' in 'ME' flipped upside down it became 'WE'. At that moment my world was flipped upside down. I was living a completely selfish life and had to make a Lane Change to live a life for others. Our mission should be to become fully servant leaders.

Do you know what event Michael Phelps' fastest personal time was when he won 8 gold medals in the Beijing Olympics? He achieved it during the team medley relay. Why? Because it wasn't about him. It was about his team. It was about the hopes and dreams of each of the other 3 teammates and honoring them in fulfilling their dreams! Talk about being a world Lane Changer!

If you want to have a vision that pulls you, pull for someone else.

Zig Ziglar says, "You will get everything you want in life if you help enough people get what they want."

Live your life in a way that becomes attractive and turns people on. When you live a life built on a foundation of the core values you have created you will begin to bring people in your life who want better for themselves because they see your lifestyle. Integrity? Passion? Happiness? Freedom? Blessing others through love and support? How could someone not want to be in your presence? And the reality is that your presence will indirectly and directly result in a better life for them. Leaders create value. Value leads to impact. And impact leads to lives changing.

This will be a process. Much like a stone, which start as rocks with rigid, jagged edges, as it moves throughout their life they get beat up, tossed around and moved across the Earth. You, Lane Changers, are those rocks today. You may have jagged edges but you are about to go on the journey to become a smooth, polished stone.

With a strong vision your reality doesn't matter. Facts don't matter. What happens to you doesn't matter. Your vision will allow you to accomplish what you want to become polished and unique.

Do you have the stones?

You are capable of Changing Lanes.

"Beyond every great challenge is a greater gift." *Savannah Ross,*

On Feb 7, 2005, Savannah was told that her 11-month old baby had less than a day to live. As if that wasn't heart wrenching enough, the previous few months had been brutal on her family. Their home caught fire at Christmas, her husband was on strike so they had no income coming in, her 6-month old niece died from cardio myopathy that same year and her son spent his first Christmas in hotel room with an exchange student.

Savannah was a makeup artist at the time, so due to her infant son's medical issues, she had to spend her days at the hospital, thus foregoing making any income. She found herself $400,000 in debt, staring down a foreclosure, a bankruptcy and a divorce. This was the proverbial rock bottom.

She needed a Lane Change.

Savannah made a decision that day that she wasn't going to let her family go without a fight. She had a toddler and a baby that was home on machines, so a traditional job wasn't going to work. She started thinking, "Who's making serious cash, and how?" Real estate investors came to mind as a legal venture and one that produces quick cash. Savannah's mom always told her that what boys can do, girls can do better. And her new career was born.

With zero experience, and within 6 months Savannah made $3.1 million dollars. Within 9 months, she became the #1 real estate investor in the nation and earned the nickname "RichMom." Currently, 6 of the top 10 investors in the country are her students. The best part? She only teaches one strategy because she's proven it works. Her belief is that you don't necessarily need to be focused on passion, you need to look at a lifestyle you want to create, and find a vehicle that will get you there. Too many of us are focused on the vehicle instead of the destination, and this leads only to unnecessary delays and roadblocks.

"Always treat others as if their potential has been realized. Watch them grow into happiness." – William Burdine

Not all of us are equipped for change—especially considering the average American would rather die than change. Restructuring your approach to life will not be easy and I won't pretend it will be. It will, in fact, be one of the hardest journeys you will ever take, but also the most rewarding. The right thing to do is often the hardest thing.

But don't be a statistic. Stand up to your insecurities and self- doubt. Beat back the voice that tells you that you can't do it. Be a maverick. Shake things up. Be bold. Don't let your past define you. And you're not alone. You have me, and my tribe, walking hand in hand with you every step of the way. We will be by your side to support you through each and every red light and stop sign you encounter along the way.

Change is tough. We all know that. But in the end, it's the greatest gift you can ever give yourself and those you love. Becoming the best version of yourself will lead you down the road to success, happiness and financial security. If you continue to keep your foot on the brake, and your eye on the rear view mirror, you fail not only those around you, but ultimately yourself. We are in this together.

Changing Lanes is a community of dynamic leaders that support and enrich the lives of others. Lane Changers respect others yet also have a great enough self-respect that they demand the same from others.

As humans, we merely see in others what we personally exhibit in our own lives.

In a society that promotes individualism, it is paramount to own who you are and love yourself unconditionally. The more you are able to admire your unique gifts and talents the more you open yourself for another person to do the same. The more you know yourself and each other, the easier it is to fully create unity. The reason is simple: when you're not focused on who you are because you are fully aware of your own value, you are able to focus and commit to being there for another person. Often, when we have not worked enough on improving ourselves – from our gifts and talents to our weaknesses and areas of improvement – we then turn to someone else and expect them to complete us. Often we do this at an unconscious level. This unspoken reality we cast upon someone else sets up both people for failure and the relationship cannot fully be cultivated.

We must go from selfishness to complete selflessness.

Remembering we only attract who we are, we must determine our boundaries.

Our key core values may differ. Determine what those are for you and do not compromise on them. Be steadfast in who you are, proud of the way you were created and open to improving yourself. The journey alone can be fun. But we are human and we crave connection. The journey with others when you are surrounded by people whose faith is solid, who passionately live life to the fullest, embrace change and are willing to grow with you and selflessly give everything to allow you to be the best you. Then the journey becomes a dream life. Changing Lanes is a journey. Where is yours leading?

PART TWO

The Impact Changing Lanes Can Have

on Your Life

"You have yet to tap into the best you."
– Darnell Davis

Lane Changers seek the opportunity to serve first and give of themselves without the expectation of receiving in return. They understand that what we reap we sow and the day is not defined by what is accomplished but by the impact that was made in the life of someone else that day. Changing Lanes is a defining movement.

Darnell knows first-hand how to first be a champion for someone else. To deliver value before ever asking for value in return, a concept that many people choose to grasp in this economic climate. A time where many are so inwardly focused and motivated, this concept goes against everything that seems to be mainstream thought. That ideal is what defines Darnell's core value.

After having some success in life

Darnell found himself one day seeking answers to questions that just did not make sense. Looking around he discovered himself alone wanting to do more with his life and a deep-rooted desire to make a bigger difference. There was only one problem. He was COMPLETELY BROKE. He was changing careers from being in the mortgage industry to building a publication after feeling the effects of the economic meltdown like many others experienced.

Excited for a Lane Change, he had the grand idea to begin a series of events named "Small Business Boot Camps" and provide business owners with an opportunity to gain valuable information that they would normally NOT have access to. As he began to build the series of seminars, his mentor wanted to come up with a value statement that would personify what their ideals were and why the events would be a dynamic opportunity for change.

After some success with the Boot Camps they decided to add this concept to other parts of their business model. The business flourished and they were blessed with more and more success. The magazine went from being just a blog to a full scale digital publication and Darnell began traveling the county sharing about Evolution Magazine. From there they had the fortune of continuing to educate people and always focused on their motto that "value differed is not value lost, rather it is stored up for just the precise moment that it would be needed."

And he saw an opportunity for a minor shift in the norm to create and entire culture for his company. The idea of the simple principle to do unto others as you would have them do unto you became a full scale digital publishing enterprise. Evolution Magazine evolved to the Evolve Media Group Inc. and went from producing one business magazine to now managing five magazine brands and publishing a host of eBooks. Evolve Media Group is geared to be a source for branding and rebranding products and services all across the country and around the planet.

Although that concept has had a profound impact on their business, it is nothing compared to the impact that it has had in Darnell's life all together. He has infused this idea into every area of his life and it has changed the way he views people, places and things. It's not an easy concept to live by because it creates vulnerability; however, when you look back and you are able "Cash In" on the value in return side of idea, what you will get is a multitude of thanks from people that you have helped in their pursuits. Even greater is the fulfillment that you will receive knowing

that you had an IMPACT on so many, your life will never be the same.

Changing Lanes can result in a completely different life for you and those who will become the beneficiary of your lifestyle.

"It's not what you know, but who you know and how you treat them." – Kent Georgi

Do you remember the people in your life who have had the biggest influence? Do you remember your favorite teacher? Can you still hear the encouraging words from that coach who pushed you to the best athlete you could be? A spiritual leader who poured into you and picked you up when you were down?

There are many assets in life but people – the right people – can be our biggest asset. People are what make life fun. People are the reason businesses thrive. The connections with people create the opportunities in life to live with a deeper purpose and mission.

One of my favorite stories is about the time when Michael Jordan scored 69 points. The Chicago Bulls' lead was so big that in the final minute Coach Phil Jackson put in Stacey King—a seldom used rookie substitute. King scored two meaningless free throws. Some years later he was asked by a reporter, "What's been the highlight of your career?" King glibly replied, "It would have to be the night Michael Jordan and I combined to score 71 points!"

Champions contribute to our success. We should be around people who make us better. The reason a lot of teams with individual all-stars win championships is because those individual players make the other players around them better. And when they come together and play like a team, they excel.

So are you playing as an individual in the game of life or are you on a winning team?

One of my mentors taught me that we become a direct reflection of the books we read and the people we hang around with the most. We must surround ourselves with people who will make us better. People who will lift our spirits. People who will allow us to dream bigger. People who will open doors for us. And if we want to continually improve and be challenged, we eventually want to have a coach or mentor who will not just tell us what we want to hear but what we need to hear.

The reality is that in life we must have powerful associations to help us have the opportunity to create that success.

Throughout my journey I've made a dedicated effort to network often and network with the right people. But I didn't always know how. Do you feel like you want to get to the next level but you're not quite sure how? Do you wonder how to get into the inner circles with the right people? I wondered the same thing.

When I first moved to San Diego, I had no job, no income and no real direction. But I knew I wanted to become successful. As I sat on the beach I noticed people having fun, enjoying nice meals, driving fancy cars and living a luxurious lifestyle. I started asking myself how? What do they know that I didn't? What do they do that I'm not? How can I have what they have?

Not having a clue or anyone to learn from, I did what I knew I needed to do.

I took action. The first step to becoming better connected is taking action by putting yourself in a position to connect with like-minded people. As a matter of fact, the best step for anything in life is taking action.

Imperfect action is better than perfect inaction.

I figured out a way to get around successful people. I went to the nicest country club in Rancho Santa Fe, a very wealthy part of San Diego, and applied to be a caddie. I was willing to do what it took to be around the financially elite. I carried their bags while they enjoyed life and I got to spend time with them. I even got paid to learn from them. I was taking their cash while filling my mental bank account. I guess you could say I was right on par.

At the end of the round I would often turn down their tips and simply thank them for enlightening me with their wisdom and guidance. They were shocked that I wasn't only there to make money and they began inviting me to grab a drink with them after the rounds in the clubhouse. I was hanging around people who had what I wanted and lived the lifestyle I wanted.

It ended up that I was there to help them but in reality they were really the ones helping me.

Every person we meet, every experience we have, every accomplishment and setback is a stepping stone to help us connect with the people who are supposed to be in our lives.

We don't always know immediately how that person will impact our life. We don't often know how we will impact theirs. But when you understand the power of connections and associations, you will look at people in a different light.

Many of the most connected people in the world suggest that "the bigger your network, the bigger your net worth."

I have learned that life is about serving. Those who serve are more fulfilled and ultimately become better connected with the premium associations.

I have had the ability, through my networking, to build an international business.

I had the ability, through my networking, to become a national bestselling author with some of the most respected people in the personal development and business world.

I have had the ability, through my networking, to be featured on the cover of national magazines.

I had the ability, through my networking, to be featured on a reality television show.

And I don't say all this to impress you. I say all this to impress UPON you the importance of networking, the importance of associations and the importance of becoming vulnerable and uncomfortable for the purpose of going to the next level.

I just mentioned some of the opportunities that have come into my life as a result of networking. But it's not about me. It's about me becoming someone who is connected enough to help others.

You are a direct reflection of the people you hang around the most.

Through my networking I've been able to help people get jobs. I've been able to help people start their own businesses. I've helped people get on blogs, television and radio shows. I've been able to refer business to other successful people. I was able to get my mentors on magazine covers and give back to them for guiding me. I've even been able to help introduce people to their soul mates.

Life is about people and I believe it is captured eloquently by the famous Bob Marley who writes "Only once in your life, I truly believe, you find someone who can completely turn your world around. You tell them things that you've never shared with another soul and they absorb everything you say and actually want to hear more. You share hopes for the future, dreams that will never come true, goals that were never achieved and the many disappointments life has thrown at you. When something wonderful happens, you can't wait to tell them about it, knowing they will share in your excitement. They are not embarrassed to cry with you when you are hurting or laugh with you when you make a fool of yourself. Never do they hurt your feelings or make you feel like you are not good enough, but rather they build you up and show you the things about yourself that make you special and even beautiful. There is never any pressure, jealousy or competition, but only a quiet calmness when they are around. You can be yourself and not worry about what they will think of you because they love you for who you are. The things that seem insignificant to most people such as a note, song or walk become invaluable treasures kept safe in your heart to cherish forever. Memories of your childhood come back and are so clear and vivid, it's like being young again. Colors seem brighter and more brilliant. Laughter seems part of daily life where before it was infrequent or didn't exist at all. A phone call or two during the day helps to get you through a long day's work and always brings a smile to your face. In their presence, there's no need for continuous conversation, but you find you're quite content in just having them nearby. Things that never interested you before become fascinating because you know they are important to this person who is so special to you. You think of this person on every occasion and in everything you do. Simple things bring them to mind like a pale blue sky, gentle wind or even a storm cloud on the horizon. You open your heart knowing that there's a chance it may be broken one day and in opening your heart, you experience a love and joy that you never dreamed possible. You find that being vulnerable is the only way to allow your heart to feel true pleasure that's so real it scares you. You find strength in knowing you have a true friend and possibly a soul mate who will remain loyal to the end. Life seems completely different, exciting and worthwhile. Your only hope and security is in knowing that they are a part of your life."

You have the opportunity to become someone of value to others. And you must have the unwavering commitment to honor yourself in becoming someone you love to be with. If you can't be happy with yourself it will be challenging to expect others to be happy around you. That may take some soul searching and introspection to determine who you are. Then you can determine who you want to become and make the necessary changes.

"Commit daily with a renewed conviction to do your best work. Be the best person you can and serve others by helping better their lives. By doing so you will receive the greatest fulfillment in life." – Jay Adkins

Their love story began in high school. Two young teens with eyes only for each other, beating the odds and getting married after college. But all was not a fairytale.

The first signs of trouble were in college when Jay began drinking heavily. It was easy to brush these incidences under the rug and label them as typical college behavior, so Annie turned a blind eye. The drinking increased and continued after graduation and the wedding.

As a loving and doting wife, Annie tried to reason with her husband when his drinking escalated, but she was met with only resistance. And being young and ill equipped to handle the rationalizations of an alcoholic, she didn't realize that every time she purchased beer at the grocery store she was enabling him, not loving him. As the drinking escalated, it was only a matter of time before disaster struck.

After a night of heavy drinking, Jay crawled into his car and attempted to drive home. Shortly thereafter he was pulled over for DUI and arrested on the side of the road. He was devastated, and so was Annie. As parents of 3 young children, she was now charged with explaining to them why daddy couldn't come home and the only way they could see him was through plexiglass. But Annie loved her husband and wanted to preserve her family, so she stood by Jay's side, certain this would be the wake-up call he needed to get his drinking under control. But alas, it was not.

Jay's drinking tapered off temporarily, but eventually picked up speed and returned to its previous levels. Annie felt at a loss as to what to do to help him. She knew it was a disease that he had no control over, and without help, would spiral out of control. She knew the edge of the cliff was nearing.

After working late into the evening, Annie returned home to a sight she thought she'd never see. The lights were blazing, the TV blaring, and the kids unbathed, but unharmed. Jay, on the other hand, was out cold from drinking himself into a stupor. He clearly had become inebriated and then passed out, leaving 3 young children unsupervised for hours. Annie was livid. This was the proverbial straw that broke the camel's back.

It was time for a Lane Change.

Jay entered inpatient rehab, which lasted 3 weeks. During this time, Annie discovered she was pregnant with their fourth child, further cementing her resolve to stand firm about his alcoholism. This was his last chance to get help and stick with it, or Annie would be forced to leave him and take the children with her. He was in no condition to be a father or a husband.

By the grace of God, Jay pulled through. After the inpatient program ended, Jay began outpatient treatment. His family rallied around him, and he not only survived, he flourished.

The real estate investing he had started dabbling in when they were first married, began to grow now that Jay had a sharp and focused mind. He was determined to build a business that would allow him financial security without taking him away from his duties as a father and husband. Jay felt his drinking had already robbed him of so much with him and he wasn't going to waste another moment.

As the business gained traction, and Jay and Annie rejuvenated their marriage, Jay realized he was being called to share his knowledge and success with others. He joined a mastermind group and began reaching out to those who have dreams as big as his. And just this year, Annie began working with Jay full time so it is now a family business.

When Jay finally hit rock bottom, he realized that Annie was his anchor and vowed to be the man he promised to be on their wedding day. And he hasn't stopped courting her since. They make a point of having date night a couple of times a month and taking weekends away without the children. They understand that what they have is a rare and special gift and so are committed to protecting and nurturing it. A couple who makes a Lane Change together, stays together.

Everything starts and ends with an attitude of gratitude.

Gratitude is a feeling or attitude in acknowledgment of a benefit that one has received or will receive.

What are you appreciative of today in your life? Are you grateful for the things you've had? Thankful for the things you currently have? Grateful for the things that are coming to you in the future?

What if you woke up tomorrow with only the things you gave thanks for today, both tangible and intangible?

How would you look at life differently starting now?

We often compare ourselves to others – the way they look, the material possessions they have, the gifts and talents they possess and the accomplishments they've had.

But you're someone who should be admired and valued as well. What things can others brag about you for? Own them! Be proud of who you are. Be confident in what you have. Express your excitement for what's coming your way and have the FAITH to know that good things are coming.

Gratitude allows us to remain humble. Gratitude also allows us to remain hungry for more and sets the barometer for what we are willing to live without and what really becomes important to us.

Every morning when I awake and every night before I fall asleep I have a GRATITUDE PARTY. That's right. I throw a party for myself twice a day giving thanks for everything I've been blessed with, including the things on that day that may not have been extremely positive.

When you begin to appreciate what you do have more things will come into your life. And you also have a heart for those who have less. Be proud of what you have. Be confident about your gifts. Don't limit yourself so others can have more, have even more so you can have what you want and provide for others. It's all about abundance – so take the last 5 letters of abundance and DANCE!! Celebrate who you are. Celebrate where you are. Celebrate who you're becoming. And celebrate where you're going.

You're blessed beyond belief.

"Every transition is an opportunity to experience greater joy and success in your life." – Stacey Ellen

The unthinkable happened to Stacey on September 20, 1999 that changed her life forever. It was a moonless rainy night, 5 streetlights were out, and a 17-year-old girl was driving without her headlights. Stacey was on a yield at an intersection and when she pulled out over the highway, the two cars collided and went into a head on collision. With no airbags in the 1989 Buick she inherited from grandma, her face and upper torso catapulted through the windshield and pulled back into the car because her seatbelt was fastened. In shock, she smelled the fuel and electrical fumes of the crash and feared the car would explode. Adrenaline pushed open the stuck car door and she fell to the pavement. Lying in the street unable to move, glass was imbedded in her face and eyes, and she was bleeding profusely. Feeling excruciating pain, she asked, "God, is this really it? Am I going to die?" A clear answer was heard, almost as if someone stood next to her, "No

Stacey, you have much more to do and accomplish in this life."

That night Stacey spent hours getting plastic surgery to repair the damage to her face, mouth, and what was left of her lips. For the next couple of years she would live with abrasions across her face and a very uneven mouth and smile. The first thing people see when they greet each other is a face and smile; therefore, each day was a continuous practice in self-love and acceptance of who she was and what she looked like. It would be years of healing thereafter for her face and smile to be that of the same girl in her high school graduation picture.

Taking a semester off from school not only gave her time to heal, but also time to slow down and reflect on life. When she looked in the mirror she not only saw a changed face but a life that needed to change.

A Lane Change often happens when we least expect it, but it's what we do with the challenges and the attitude we choose in our circumstances, that dictates how our life will unfold.

Months passed and Stacey was determined to finish college. Life seemed different than it had in the past. Her interest in partying non-stop and hanging with the same group of friends stopped. For the first time in her life she got straight A's and graduated on the honor roll. She trusted there was a greater reason for her survival and was determined to discover her passion and life-path. Although she has healed most of the emotional and physical scars related to her accident, she continues to live with visible scars on her face. These scars don't define her, but remind her to always share joy and love with others no matter who they are, what they look like, or what they may be going through.

Although nothing has been the same since the accident, the positives out-weighed the negatives and she now sees the lessons and growth that resulted from the experience. It takes determined self–introspection and self–love to journey inward. Life is a journey and not a destination to self-discovery; there will always be more to examine and clear. We are not defined by our past, we can create and experience joy and self-love on a daily basis.

After college Stacey's goal was to live and "make it" in the big city of Chicago, then move to the West Coast. She moved to Chicago after the terrorist attack of 2001 and set sail in a dead economy. Determined to find employment, she landed different jobs and eventually was living out the life that others had wanted for her. Growing up she was taught success meant getting a "real corporate job", make lots of money, and gain approval of others. For years she worked her way up the corporate later helping others build their businesses and become successful. She eventually helped build 5 different companies and was able to buy a nice car, condo, and was making over 6 figures. Everyone around her thought she was happy and congratulated her for her success, but inside she was miserable, lonely, and had no life balance.

Challenges and disappointments are part of life but they do not define our lives. The practice of patience and continuous self-love allows joy to abound under any circumstance.

Stacey felt her life was crumbling in Chicago; so she decided to make an intentional Lane Change and move to her favorite city on the West Coast, San Diego. Her reoccurring visions to own a business that helped others continued to grow and develop. Growing up Stacey was introduced to personal development at a young age with loving parents who believed in her and wanted the best. However, sometimes we get caught living the life everyone else thinks we should lead, rather than finding our own way uncovering our own unique talents, passions, and purpose. At one point in your life I'm sure you asked yourself, "Why am I here?" or "What am I here to do?"

Sometimes we have to physically move from our home, our city, or our place of employment in order open our minds and our hearts to new ways of living, thinking, and being. When we take a step out of our comfort zone we open ourselves up to experiencing greater joy and seeing all that's possible. If we keep a healthy attitude of joy and expectation we find the courage to trust our higher power and make moves to further develop our personalities, jobs, friendships and passions.

They often say, "When someone is ready, the teacher will appear." Over the next few years in San Diego Stacey sought healers, teachers, spiritual guides, and business mentors to assist along her path of further self-discovery in becoming an entrepreneur. In this space she insisted on intentionally creating her life no matter what the circumstance. The goal was to do things that felt aligned with her values and love of helping others. It didn't matter what was happening in her life, she kept moving forward practicing being led by her heart. She felt push back from parents and friends, but she let go of others negativity around stepping outside of the typical corporate work environment.

Leaving the comfort of working for others she got a roommate for the first time in years and went broke attempting to figure out her future. Kneeling down against her bed she would pray for assistance as she cried and searched for answers. It wasn't until she trusted that she was on the right path, and took action toward her vision did everything became clear.

When we are open, raw, and trusting that all will unfold according to divine timing, everything will eventually be revealed to us. When we ask for what we want, trust it is possible, and believe we are worthy, all of our desires will unfold.

After healing more of her own insecurities and fears, she realized that she had to experience the frustration and confusion, to eventually find the clarity she sought. It was through all of the trials and tribulations that she would grow, expand, and realize that she had healing gifts within that were being refined throughout her entire life journey.

We all experience Lane Changes through life. We reach clarity when we take time to understand our strengths and unique gifts we have to share with the world. The answers are always within and will unveil themselves if we practice connecting with our heart, intuition, and remain open to all possibilities that are around us.

Manuals and self-help books may serve a purpose, but they do not give the human validation, and comfort or support we need to make changes in our lives. A mentor or someone that offers guidance and accountability are invaluable in meeting life's Lane Changes.

Today Stacey is living her passion and helps people all over the world connect to their joy and intentionally create the life of their dreams. As the creator of Joy to Success, she finds her clients are the most creative, powerful, and successful when they are connected to their joy within. She works with a variety of people going through career or life transitions to mentoring those in business providing strategies to double their business revenue.

Lane Changes can help you move from simply surviving to thriving in the life you always dreamt of living. Know that you are worthy of success and believe it's possible. Be bold, be willing to do the work, and remain open to the possibilities that exist around you.

How can you thrive through your own Lane Changes? How can you use your Lane Changes to intentionally create the life of your dreams?

Changing lanes is a cross-country trip with the windows down and the music blaring. It takes time, but the destination is reachable. And once you arrive, you will understand what all of those long hours were for. Hard work pays off, despite the rush hour traffic and construction zones that may delay your progress. But these are temporary setbacks that, with perseverance, will be overcome.

Change is a catalyst that can turn your life upside down—for the better. Once you have decided that you long for and NEED more than the status quo, you will experience a level of insight and clarity once denied to you. The breakthrough will open up the floodgates of ideas that have been trapped inside of you for far too long.

Becoming a Lane Changer will not only change your life, but will impact the lives of everyone around you. You can move through life with confidence, reaching out to help others who are in the wrong lane. You'll be asked "What happened to you?" and you can answer, "I CHANGED LANES!"

Changing Lanes vs Cruise Control

Life is not about what you accomplish while you live, but how you live in your accomplishments.

We often go through life aspiring to be like someone we admire because of what they have accomplished. The reality is they just pushed a little harder, dreamed a little bigger and kept going when most others would give up.

The two most important things we have in this world are relationships and time. The better relationships we build with the right people the more fulfilled our lives will become. The more we fully live our lives enjoying each precious moment with the time we have been gifted, the more satisfied we will be.

Life is not about what we do as much as it is how we do it, why we do it and who we impact along the journey.

Challenges will come up. Frustration is inevitable. Loss is certain. Stress is unavoidable. But success...success is up to you. It's not up to your spouse; not up to your business partner; not up to your friend; not your team; not anyone but you.

I will stand on my own Championship podium knowing that I was defeated and got back up, that I was battered and bruised and ridiculed but pushed even harder, that I was made fun of and joked about but I was the one who was laughing at the end. When I look back at all of the pain, the hurt, the anguish, the ups and downs and defeat, the misery and embarrassment, the frustration and disappointment...I will stand proudly knowing that I didn't give up, that I persevered long enough to taste victory and that all of the tangible rewards pale in comparison to the person I became in the process – that I became a Lane Changer.

The game of life not about losing or winning – it's about becoming.

One of the worst things we can do to ourselves is cruise through life on easy street, never stepping out of our comfort zones. Growth and evolution only occur in the throws of discomfort and conflict within ourselves. We have to feel the pain in order to evolve as human beings. Masking our emotions will only delay the inevitable.

Driving through life on cruise control with the wind blowing through your hair may seem ideal, and it is in short periods. But to adopt this as a philosophy for life, will most certainly wreak havoc. It will put you in the fast lane to misery and you will be stuck on the side of the road indefinitely. Cruise control is fraught with potholes and lane closures disguised as shortcuts. Don't be fooled.

Changing lanes takes time, dedication, effort and commitment, but ultimately provides an inner peace and satisfaction with oneself that supersedes settling for easy street. Don't let fear hold you back from living the life you were meant to live. So many of us make the mistake of listening to a world that tells us we're not good enough and will never be anything more than what we are today, but this is a lie. YOU DESERVE BETTER, and if you stick with it, you'll discover the road map that leads to unlocking your true potential.

Are You Ready to Change Lanes?

"To stay small to protect someone's ego is a disservice to all. Choose to be with people who bring out the best in you." - Ferlie Almonte

Preparation and perseverance will be your friends through this journey. Change is unachievable without the proper mindset. You must embrace the unknown, not fear it. There are no shortcuts, but there is a well-worn path to lead you that has been walked by those who have come before you. Our tribe will be your designated drivers, ensuring you avoid the detours and distractions along the way.

As with all changes in life, those who feel left behind will be your biggest detractors. Their selfishness and insecurities will prevent them from supporting you for fear they no longer measure up. When someone first said misery loves company, they weren't exaggerating. Like attracts like, meaning there will inevitably be some collateral damage, and you must be prepared for this. Friendships are not always life-long, and we often outgrow each other—and that's ok. There are people who come into our lives for a season and some for a lifetime...don't confuse the two.

Are you ready, willing and able to take the next step? If so, buckle up, because it's going to be the ride of your life!

PART THREE

"Don't wait for the Rescue, because you are the Rescue." *Scott Lopez*

Good things come to those who wait. Wrong. Good things come to those who go after what they want with everything they've got. There is no secret passageway to success that allows you to skip all of the closed roads and detours. It's good, old-fashioned hard work that will lead you to who you are meant to become. Don't cheat yourself by taking shortcuts—you're wasting your time as you'll only be driving in circles. But hard work isn't necessarily the magic bullet. You have to show up and grow up to go up.

If you can commit to put in the time and the effort, you will get to the finish line of this crazy road trip called life with a sense of peace and accomplishment. Don't be afraid of hard work—it pays off in spades. I've gone from someone who didn't know his calling or passion, to someone who actually gets paid to do what he loves. And I want this for you.

Do you have what it takes to change lives—including your own? Do you long for a life of peace and fulfillment? Do you have the mindset to blaze a trail into the future?

Lane Changers are from all walks of life and come in all shapes and sizes. No matter your past or your present, we are a tribe of helpers and doers. We don't sit idly by and watch our fellow tribesmen drive off the road into a ditch. We're a community, a family, and we behave as such. Bottom line, we're in this together.

Deciding to become a Lane Changer will be a defining moment in your life. It will take a tremendous amount of focus and will require your 100% commitment. It won't happen overnight, but good things generally don't. It's a consistent effort and a pattern of smart decisions that lead to a permanent Lane Change. Shifting temporarily is an exercise in futility. There's simply no point. Lane Changers are lifers and we go all in.

The Lane Change Will Be Your Game Changer.

The effects of changing lanes will reverberate throughout every aspect of your life. No stone will be left unturned. Your career, your family, your friends, your spirituality, and your health will all be affected. This will be one of those life changing experiences that will be seared into your memory forever.

You will feel happier, even peaceful, and experience the essence of true joy, which will be a first for many of you. Gone are the days of toiling away in the same dead end mindset that led nowhere. You will be a part of a revolution that will take you to places you never thought possible. The status quo will no longer satisfy you, as you will thrive on your newfound passions and accomplishments. Changing lanes is the road trip of a lifetime!

How to Change Lanes ?

Show up, Grow up and Go up. That is the 'secret' to success. There is no quick fix, or get-rich-quick scheme. You have to show up every day and put in the hard work necessary to change lanes. And growing up is a big part of this process. Where you are in life is a direct result of the choices YOU have made, and the responsibility for where you go from here rests squarely on your shoulders. You will never 'go up' if you stay stuck in the quagmire of the past, blaming everyone but yourself for where you are.

When you become a Lane Changer and rid yourself of the weight of your past disappointments, you will understand why the rearview mirror is smaller than the windshield. We need to look back to learn, but don't get stuck there. What we think about, we bring about. As we look forward at the road ahead, we're able to focus on where we want to go instead of where we've been.

People will notice and ask about your secret. Co-workers will wonder what makes you so special. Family will scratch their heads in wonder. And you can tell them how simple it really is— you swerved into the fast lane, cutting off those who tried to hold you back.

You'll see how your mindset will change your view of every situation you encounter. You will come to view obstacles as opportunities, roadblocks as entrance ramps and potholes as windows to growth.

And often we put others ahead of ourselves. And that's great. But we also much take the responsibility to make ourselves a priority.

"You may enjoy life this way or that, but it's much more fulfilling when you've had an active role in what happens. Take responsibility and live your life on purpose!" – Rob Campbell

The relationships we have in our lives can often cause a lot of turmoil and can take years to grow from. Yet the chance for growth comes from an age-old principle; "out of every adversity comes opportunity".

Often we have Lane-Changing moments that determine where we end up – not necessarily by our choices but the circumstances into which we were born. Rob Campbell's parents divorced when he was 13, leaving him in a position many have faced and like many, he experienced one of his defining moments early in life. Rob didn't face that reality lightly. His reality was determined by circumstances out of his control and how he reacted to that reality was up to him.

Usually these types of circumstances force us to grow. We can look outside of our circumstances for resources and ways of change, yet it's a matter of commitment to ourselves whether we choose to grow. We can either be defined by our circumstances or produce new ones creating an entirely new reality. New relationships form through our adversities and consequently, as a result of his parent's decisions, new relationships became possible and old ones were being put through the "fire of life".

One of the significant things about his parent's divorce was that Rob was able to seize the moment most would have missed because they were looking at the situation rather than the opportunity. He did what he knew and that was using his natural gifts and talents to take a next step. He went to train with the Olympic luge team and he found himself away from home for months at a time. There he formed relationships with other athletes and coaches and he learned from his coaches about the commitment it takes to become a champion. He quickly learned to be independent and at age 14 he was responsible for many things like raising money, schoolwork, training and developing his relationships. He created the future he wanted based on the Lane Change he made as a result of the circumstances that were forced upon him. How many times have we been cut off in life and curse the other person? How many times have you thought that circumstances were derailing you from your ultimate purpose? Sometimes we harbor strong emotions of anger, resentment, bad experiences, and rage rather than redirecting it for a greater good.

Rob had a skill that he realized could teach him more than just academics. He was resilient, resourceful and unwilling to settle for less than the greatness he expected of himself. Using his God-given athletic abilities, Rob went to the national tryouts for the United States Luge Junior Development team with 120 other competitors. Just 2 months later he found himself among only 12. His determination, drive, persistence, work ethic and ability to tap into that fire that he felt when his parents divorced fueled his competitive spirit. The following year he was

National team candidate and more importantly than the title was the accomplishment he felt. He stood on the podium of life with a medal around his neck that signified more than bronze, silver or gold – it represented the "blood, sweat and tears" of his childhood. Talk about Changing Lanes!

Rob and his dad always had an amazing relationship despite their unique differences. Eventually, Rob went to work for his dad's business and during those formative years he learned skills of entrepreneurship and leadership that would come to serve him later in life.

The beauty in the whole situation is Rob was also able to learn a lot from his mom who was also an entrepreneur and had a deep-rooted faith. They were able to connect spiritually together with that strength that comes from those close bonds and belief in God. He always believed deeply that Jeremiah 29:11 promises "plans to prosper you and not to harm you, plans to give you hope and a future." Their relationship was built on a solid rock and together they have supported each other through the good and the bad. His mom loves Rob unconditionally and always wanted the best for him. She always encouraged and inspired him.

Rob was the oldest of three and desired to be an example, a counselor and a leader. Relationships become one of the greatest influences in our lives – for the good or the bad. Who we surround ourselves with will shape who we become. Sometimes we have the ability to choose our surroundings while others are chosen for us. Every relationship needs to be continually examined so that we can make the appropriate Lane Changes needed to effectively pursue our goals and fulfill our ultimate purpose. The relationships that do not push us to greatness need to become minimal and possibly even done away with entirely.

That entrepreneurial drive Rob gained from his mom and dad led him to go back to school. During his years in college and playing competitive ice hockey, he picked up the thrill of gambling. Through his ups and downs

Rob learned some valuable life and financial lessons. Specifically, Rob realized you can't win by gambling. Yet many of us gamble our lives away in our relationships, dead-end jobs, our health and our spiritual choices that set us up to become bankrupt emotionally and physically. Living a life in financial debt is challenging but living life in debt to yourself by not going after life with all you've got is the biggest debt one can hold.

His decisions led him down a different road and Rob entered the corporate world. He became excited about the vision of a life it would provide. He quickly began chasing titles, status and achievement based on someone else's standards. He also ended up looking to others for a sense of accomplishment. What he realized is that chasing other people's dreams became very restrictive. His vision of corporate America didn't live up to the reality it provided and he longed for what he had with his dad. While his dad worked really hard, he still had freedom to make choices that fit life into his work rather than have work design his life or not. He had lost his idea of freedom in the cubicle and wanted to be able to create his life by design rather than have someone else design his life for him. Rob continually reminds himself "I would rather live inspired in pursuit of a dream, than dream to work a lifetime losing hope".

Being an entrepreneur has allowed Rob to truly value of productive friendships.

People in his world now support him and are interested in mutual success compared with his experience in corporate America where it seemed that most are competing against each other and people looking after themselves rather than looking out for each other collectively. Each person we have in our lives shapes us and the decisions we make based on those relationships determine our future. The power and importance of picking, developing and refining relationships cannot be underestimated.

Continually investing in his personal growth, Rob carries with him many teachings from his coaches and mentors. He understands that there is always someone better than you and it's important to humble yourself and learn from them. Especially in team building it's also important to recognize others strengths and then utilize them towards a common goal. Personal strengths can also be assets to others if we choose to share them and be the teacher for those that seek you as a friend and mentor. Rob truly resonated with Jim Rohn who suggests that "If you don't design your own life plan, chances are you'll fall into someone else's plan. And guess what they have planned for you? Not much."

Rob has used that entrepreneurial competitive spirit, team unity, and collaborative dynamic to build an international business. He has always had the desire to learn. But what separates him is that he applies the knowledge he gains. It's said that "Ignorance on fire is better than knowledge on ice." But Rob spent his childhood on ice and realizes that knowledge on fire, combined with the right relationships, will ignite an entire possibility unimagined by the average person.

Relationships are not just about "us", they are also about "we", and one of the greatest satisfactions in life is when you can take an experience or "lesson learned" from your relationships, then turn that into an experience or life lesson for someone else and see the positive impact it has in the life of others. It's important that we emphasize the good experiences and pass them along but an even greater impact is taking the bad and using it for good.

It's time to plan your work and work your plan. It's time to foster and form your best relationships. Repair those that are broken, cut off the ones that hold you back, and plant the seeds to new ones that will help you reach your God-given potential. Your road to greatness will not be travelled alone; it must be paved not just with good intentions but direction, drive, determination and quality people. The team you surround yourself with will contribute to the actions you take to achieve the results you desire. Give your best to yourself, and those around you.

It's time for you to Change Lanes!

Priorities establish your focus; your focus determines your actions; and your actions will ultimately become the results you get in life.

When your priorities are aligned, your life will have balance. When your priorities are off, your life becomes a little more dysfunctional.

I remember when I was getting started in business, my priorities were completely skewed. I was so focused on making money, that everyone I talked to most likely felt like they had a target on their chest. I looked at people as dollar signs rather than as, well, people. My relationships started to struggle. My business didn't grow. And ultimately I got frustrated and lost focus. Therefore, my actions were inconsistent and my results sent my life in a downward spiral.

Where are you priorities? Perhaps it's important first to look at your values.

When you want someone to think of you, how do you want them to describe you? What are your values? Are you living your life in such a way to honor your values or do you need to change some of your behaviors?

Often we attract what we are or what we believe we deserve. I wanted to attract the people with traits I thought were important to creating success, yet I didn't possess those myself. The disconnect created a big separation. So I went to work on myself.

I looked at my life and started reflecting on what was important. When I looked at my life I realized my priorities were "F"ed Up!! So I came up with the "F"ormula for Success in my life. I would challenge you to determine what aspects of life are important to you and begin to increase your score in each of those areas.

My "F"s are:

Faith

Family

Fitness

Friendships

Fun

Finances

And yes, in that order. Well, Fun is pervasive in each one of the other areas but I also set specific time to have fun and live life doing what I love.

Now remember, what we focus on is what we will attract in our life. So I am not telling you to ignore the areas in your life that are important. If you completely ignore those areas they will most likely disappear. I am simply challenging you to determine if your priorities are in the right order.

Again, the important areas in my life have been focused on:

Faith – It is fair to say that we all believe in something greater than ourselves. I know where my faith is and where my religious beliefs lie. And in my life faith is a very important aspect of my success and I believe because of my faith all of the other areas of my life are strong. However, if you are not a religious person you still must find a

faith – Something you can believe in that keeps you going and helps you fulfill that desire to create something bigger than yourself.

Family – This is the backbone of my life and the reason I do a lot of what I do. I understand that not everyone has the healthiest relationship with their biological family. Perhaps you can take a look at that and see if you can patch up those relationships. If you have a solid relationship with your family lean on them to stay blessed. If you don't have a biological family that you appreciate, I challenge you to create another family – a group of people who unconditionally love and support you in your visions, dreams and goals. We need a support system and your "family" will be a key part in getting you where you want to go.

Fitness – Your body is a temple and you should treat it that way; most people treat it like the Temple of DOOM. There have been numerous studies that prove wealthy people are healthy people. There is a strong correlation between physical fitness and fiscal fitness. Why? Because when your body is operating an elite level, your work ethic improves, your cognitive ability increases and your energy levels are high enough to accomplish what you need in your business. Additionally, exercise decreases stress levels which allow neurotransmitters to increase creativity and productivity. It is absolutely essential to incorporate wellness and physical fitness into your daily routine. Your pants size and your bank account will thank you.

Friendships – People are what make this world go round. It is critical that you have a social life. It keeps you sane, allows you to have fun, makes work worth it when you can play hard with buddies and good friends can speak truth into your life.

Fun – You have to find time to have fun. Work hard, play hard baby!! If you're fortunate enough to have a business you love and have fun doing than you will never work another day in your life. When you're working, work. When you're having fun, have fun. Learn to separate the two. Often, people bring work home with them and are always worried about what they need to do. When you're done working, start having fun. When you're having fun, don't think about work. Life is designed to be a blast. Don't miss out on life – it's so much better when you're actually living it!

Finances – Money is necessary. The more you have the more options you have. But money is not everything. It's a means to enjoy the life you want to live. We all need money, but none of us need money to control our lives. Control your priorities and your finances will take care of themselves.

Lane Changers live abundant lives, not just financially but in all areas of life. Yet when I was broke I realized the worst thing about being broke was not having a surplus to provide others with their needs.

So I discovered more about what my beliefs are around money and found that I had a focus on scarcity rather than abundance.

We have talked a lot about the mindset behind creating success. As we know from many thought leaders that the key to financial freedom starts with your belief in the ability to create it. Money is nothing more than tangible object exchanging hands.

However, each of our belief systems around money is based upon a set of beliefs formed by our circumstances, those who we were taught by and our experiences. So are you consciously aware of your unconscious beliefs about money? In other words, are you aware of how you view money? At the mere mention of the word "MONEY" what thoughts come to mind? Positive or negative? Why is that? Was it a taboo subject in your family and your parents never talked about it? Or did the people in your life when you were growing up educate you about money and talk openly about it?

Through my journey into appreciating wealth I have a completely different view than I used to. Reading books about money, hanging out with people who have money and looking at my bank account, realizing what I was doing wasn't working, forced me to shift my paradigm. The first book that opened my mind to the idea of understanding money was "Rich Dad, Poor Dad" by Robert Kiyosaki. And in that book he explains the difference between the various opportunities to make money.

As a teacher in the public school I was teaching young minds how to fill in a scantron, to get good grades, to become a good student which was setting them up to become a good employee. And I wasn't OK with that. Why? Well I didn't believe in that methodology any longer so why would I teach our future generations what I didn't believe. The same way I hope you can look at your financial situation and determine if you need to go back to the school again – except this time you get to pick the information you learn. Noam Chomsky brilliantly says, "Students who acquire large debts putting themselves through school are unlikely to think about changing society. When you trap people in a system of debt they can't afford the time to think. Tuition fees increases are disciplinary technique, and by the time students graduate, they are not only loaded with debt, but have also internalized the disciplinarian culture. This makes them efficient components of the consumer economy."

Now don't hear what I'm not saying. I believe in education and I believe in higher education. I graduated from a top university with a 3.4 GPA. What I am suggesting is that being a highly educated person in academia doesn't necessarily translate into to the lifestyle they are able to create.

How many highly educated people do you know right now who are struggling financially? On the contrary, how many uneducated people do you know who are driving nice cars, living in dream homes and living lifestyle anyone who wants money would desire?

If you want what you want you may have to do things you're not. The old school ways of making a living may not be the best. Now if it's working for you continue doing what you're doing. And maybe consider adding something to what you're doing. If what you're doing is not working perhaps you should subtract something that's not working and redirect your focus to something that can create what you want. You may need a financial Lane Change.

Jim Rohn, one of the most well respected personal development and business leaders of our time said, "Education will make you a living. Self-education will make you a fortune."

This awareness in my life not only helped me look at money differently but it also helped me earn differently. Additionally, it forced me into becoming uncomfortable which has led me to start businesses, have the ability to travel, and impact lives along the journey.

Again, keep in mind as we unpack the reality of your financial situation that there are things we know we know; there are things we know we don't know; and there are things we don't know we don't know.

The choice becomes are you willing to learn something that will help you? If so, are you willing to do the things necessary to make your new teachings

put more money into your bank
account?

Great!

There are key attributes that many financially successful people accept as truth. I want to share with you the Lane Changers formula for W.E.A.L.T.H. – the principles based upon what I've learned from wealthy people as well as from my own personal ups and downs in business.

The first principle in create **W.E.A.L.T.H.** is

Work your butt off

Every single person who has made their own money works really, really freaking hard. Now there are obviously different ways to make money and you can establish systems and other techniques to make making money easier, but no matter what, you will always find financially well off people working hard. There really is no other way around it. If you want money, you have to work for it. I simply challenge you to find ways to make easier money so that you hard work pays you a higher ROI.

One way to do that is to start a business or join a business model that is an

Expanding market

Going against the stream is often challenging and tiring. While there are huge opportunities in this and there are times where you shouldn't follow the masses, there is also an understanding that doing what others are doing successfully can result in prosperity for us. Figure out where the money is going and be there for it to come to you. And if you're going to work really freaking hard and be involved in making money in a way that gives you a higher chance of doing that, it's important to build

Assets

What is an asset? Well, simply it's something that continues to make you money. A liability, on the other hand, is something that costs you money. So an important key to creating wealth is to build assets. So focus your time, attention and energy on something that is building YOUR portfolio, not just someone else's future.

And if you can apply the next principle to what you're currently doing OR implement it into a new vehicle for making money you will have the ability to do more with your time. It's called:

Leverage

J Paul Getty, the world's first billionaire said, "I'd rather make 1% of 100 people's efforts than 100% of my own."

So theoretically when you create leverage you should be able to earn an income that's not tied to your personal investment of time. It's known as leveraged income.

Understanding the principle of empowering others to help you, it is paramount to create a

Team

We know the importance of utilizing the skills and time of others. It will be vital for you to not just leverage your time and money but to also leverage people.

Work your strengths and hire your weaknesses.

And finally, in the Lane Changer's WEALTH formula, you MUST, especially in today's society:

Have Multiple Streams of Income

Lane Changers should be creating a new stream of residual income every year.

So there you go. Is the only formula that makes sense? Of course not. It's what I have created and used to help me start working toward becoming wealthy and through teaching others it has allowed them to do the same.

And remember, money is not everything. But it certainly helps having more of it. So wherever your current financial situation is today realize it doesn't have to remain your reality. It is paramount to do a reality check because if not most of your actual checks may bounce.

When it comes to our bodies we go to a doctor and get a physical.
I also recommend from a personal development standpoint you do a checkup from the neck up.
And when it comes to building wealth, the first step may be doing to have a financial physical.

How many of these principles resonate with you:

Work Hard?
Evolving business?

Assets?

Leverage?

The Power of Residual Income?

Having Multiple Streams?

If you know where you want to go you're off to a good start. If you have a plan to get there you're off to a better start. If you take the right action, consistently to actually make your goals a reality than perhaps you will be one of the fortunate people to create wealth.

Don't just chase your dreams...catch them!!

You are the creator of your life moving forward.

So what's the answer? Changing Lanes.

As George Clason writes in 'The Richest Man in Babylon,'
"Ahead of you stretches your future like a road leading into the distance. Along that road are ambitions you wish to accomplish . . . desires you wish to gratify.

To bring your ambitions and desires to fulfillment, you must be successful with money. Use the financial principles made clear in the pages which follow.

Let them guide you away from the stringencies of a lean purse to that fuller, happier life a full purse makes possible. Like the law of gravity, they are universal and unchanging. May they prove for you, as they have proven to so many others, a sure key to a fat purse, larger bank balances and gratifying financial progress."

But here's the reality…

It's challenging. It's different from what most people understand. It takes a delayed gratification approach. It's a process. And it's not for everybody. And that's OK.

It's time to become a Lane Changer and not just a WANTrepreneur – someone who wants a better life, more money, more time freedom and the ability to create a legacy but unwilling to go all in. If you're going to get where you want to go it will take a true commitment. These will be required:

1) Confidence

The ability to accurately know yourself and the courage to step out into greatness is fundamental. People won't understand what you're doing. They will think you're crazy. They will discount your talents. They will undermine your value. But guess what? You won't care because you know that you want a different life than they are living. To become a truly empowered entrepreneur it takes full dedication to yourself as well as your dreams. Through the challenges life will throw you as you courageously build a business, you will become a different person; you will become a leader. And with humble pride and the unequivocal enthusiasm you will need, the confidence to achieve success no matter what cost will benefit you as potentially the greatest attribute as an entrepreneur.

2) Independently motivated with a team

Everyone who is building a business for some monetary reasons wants to become wealthy. The more I surround myself with unbelievably successful people, the more I realize they got to where they are by surrounding themselves with people better than them. The concept "Self–made millionaire" is a misconception. They personally may be the millionaire as a result of their hard work but they had to have others help them along the journey. That way you can achieve more with a team that is focused on accomplishing the mission together and is willing to come alongside you because of your vision.

3) Relationship Builder

Many successful people admit that you're "Network is your Net Worth." Becoming a person of influence is vital to expanding your business. The more people you affect and the more influential those people are to society, the more you open yourself to powerful potential. As you serve others they will want to support you. By building relationships you design yourself as someone who others want to be around. Then you can align yourself with people in power positions. Then you can define your purpose and position yourself as an authority. Relationships are everything in personal life as well as professional life. The person that establishes the best relationships with those who can help them get where they want to go will ultimately have the most options and options create opportunities. Become a person of value and service and you will reach new levels of entrepreneurship that others will admire and strive to surround themselves with you.

4) Business Focus

FOCUS stands for Follow One Course Until Successful. Too often we chase after too many things and don't have success at any of them. I have certainly fallen victim to "Shiny Object Syndrome." That being said, I do believe there is power in getting experience in different endeavors to learn, grow, expand your network and determine where you want your focus to be. However, if you continue to do this day in and day out, month after month you will find that you're no further ahead then you were when you started but with a lot more frustration. Go after what you want with all you've got. When you've achieved a certain level of success then you can determine if you want to keep going in that direction or if you've establish yourself enough to take on the next challenge in a new endeavor. Do one thing great rather than a lot of things mediocre. You deserve it.

5) Determination

Vince Lombardi says, "The difference between a successful person and others is not a lack of strength, not a lack of knowledge, but rather a lack in will." If you ask successful entrepreneurs what helped them achieve their level of greatness one of the most unanimous themes is 'Stickability.' They were resilient, relentless and pushed harder when times got tough. Chuck Yeager broke the sound barrier because he was willing to keep pushing harder than any other man who had attempted before him. He wasn't necessarily any more suitable to achieve that record, he was just more determined. You're going to experience times where you will want to quit. You will be ready to throw in the towel. You will question why you are doing everything you are, and at that point you need to remember why you started in the first place and reach down deeper than you ever have and commit to the cause. Your cause; your life and your dreams.

So what makes me suitable to share these strategies with you? I'm a National Bestselling author, rose to top of a real estate investment firm being the youngest to achieve the level I reached and am currently building a business that has expanded in 5 countries. And I've lost 63 pounds and know that everything we do takes these same principles in our professional as well as our personal life. I don't say this to impress you but instead to impress upon you the importance of going after what you want with everything you have.

A mentor and coach tells you want you need to hear, not just want you want to hear. These steps will support you during your journey and that's exactly what this is; a marathon, not a sprint

so take the first step or the next step

and keep going strong!!

Remember the key to living a fulfilled and happy life is having balance. Learn what motivates you. What drives you? What makes you full of joy? Are you doing those things every day? If not, why not? Then change your priorities. If you are doing those things everyday keep going. You're on a great path.

There comes a point in every man's life when he has to look himself in the mirror and figure out who he is. When you can learn what makes you happy, what makes you tick, what makes you who you were created to be, life is a lot more fun. Dream BIG, work hard, prioritize your life, live passionately and help as many people along the way do the same. That's what life is about my friends. And you are a champion so go live a world class life!!

And never, ever, ever, ever, ever, ever, ever, ever compromise. That's right. I know all relationships are built around compromise and without it the relationship will die. But the most powerful relationship you have is with yourself and I'm telling you NEVER COMPROMISE.

NEVER COMPROMISE on your core values. Your core values will forever guide you in every decision. I'm not suggesting that every decision you make will confirm your core values, but every decision will help you shape and confirm who you truly embody. Too often we know who we are and who we want to be but we cross the boundary to see what it will feel like on the other side.

My biggest setbacks, struggles and challenges all were a result of going against my core values. It got me in a lot of trouble.

Ultimately, I was able to reflect on that decision and realize who I truly am and that the decision I made didn't align with my core values. I compromised.

I have decided that I will never compromise on my core values again. It doesn't mean I won't make another mistake it simply means that I'm not willing to change who I am because of external influences, other people's opinions, or worldly circumstances. I won't compromise.

And you want to know the truth? I've lost a lot of money because of my core values. I've been made fun of because of my core values. I've missed out on life-changing opportunities because of my core values. I've lost friends because of my core values. But guess what? The experiences I've had as a result of my core values are priceless and the doors of opportunity that will open because of my unwavering commitment to my core values will far trump any of those things I've lost. Faith honors honorable people. That's right, while sometimes the good guys finish last, at least they will finish with pride, a deep respect for themselves and ultimately win the respect of everyone else. I won't compromise.

Take a look at the word 'compromise.' Do you see the letters in the middle?

PRO. I am continuing to become a PRO at being me; a pro at committing to myself and my core values; a pro at deciding who I want to be, how I want to represent my legacy.

Do not compromise.

You are a LANE CHANGER!

L ifestyle and Legacy – Your story is powerful and you should use it to transform lives, create a legacy and help others create their own legacy.

A cknowledgement – People will work for money but they will die for respect and recognition. Build a team. Praise them. Help them become Lane Changers.

N obody cares about what you say. Rather than just tell people what you are going to do, go out and show them.

E lation – People enjoy being around happy people. Become so exultant that others wonder what is different about you.

C ourage – Realize it is a journey and taking the first step can often be the hardest. This is your time, your opportunity and your turn to impact the world.

H eart-centered – We don't affect people as much by what we say or do;

we affect them by the way we make them feel. Lead with your heart and serve unconditionally.

A bsolute dedication – Those who have achieved success have given it all they've got. You can accomplish anything you want as long as you're willing to do whatever it takes for as long as it takes.

N obility – The biggest differentiator is the level of integrity you live with. Give people the reason to only talk positively about you because you do things with unwavering core values.

G ifts and Talents – You are unique and you were designed to provide the world with what only you can. Be bold about your brilliance and proud about your aptitudes.

E veryone who has what you want and is where you want to be, has been through what you will go through to get it. Let your vision lead you through the challenges.

R esponsibility – You are responsible for your own future. You are also responsible for the future of those you want to create a legacy for. You are a Lane Changer.

Life is not a dress rehearsal. – *Sonya Berg*

What's Next as a Lane Changer?

"There are two basic motivating forces: fear and love. When we are afraid, we pull back from life. When we are in love, we open to all that life has to offer with passion, excitement, and acceptance. We need to learn to love ourselves first, in all our glory and our imperfections. If we cannot love ourselves, we cannot fully open to our ability to love others or our potential to create. All hopes for a better world rest in the fearlessness and open-hearted vision of people who embrace life." – John Lennon

The future to most is scary and full of unknowns, but to Lane Changers, the future is where dreams are made. The reality is that your journey may seem overwhelming and daunting at times, but successful people continue pushing ahead despite not having all the answers. Does your future seem dark and the unknown thwarts any movement in your life? Headlights do not show us 10 miles ahead, but illuminate what's right in front of us. This allows us to continue moving forward so we make progress towards our destination. The same concept applies to Lane Changers. The point is not to know the future, but to be focused and aware enough to progress forward without swerving off the road.

Growth and progress become evident and excitement builds. It's our light at the end of the tunnel and it's what keeps us holding on when we fear we're at our breaking point.

As a Lane Changer, the future is our holy grail. And not just our own. The futures of those around us are also positively impacted by our choices today to take a leap of faith, jump in the car and get on the road.

Ultimately, our mindset determines our destiny and our actions determine our future.

Lane Changers have the opportunity to use the carpool lane on the road to success. Our tribe works together, grows together and our mentors help ease the strain of congestion along the way. My purpose in writing this is to give you the fast pass, so you don't have to take the same detours I did along the way. We all have different vehicles, but the destination is the same and others will want to come along for the ride.

We are all destined to create living legacies for those in our lives. The problem is that most of us are too focused on what are going to do today to simply survive. Often, we lead lives of survival rather than lives of abundance. When we are able to move from the desire just to survive to the desire to thrive we have so much more to share with others.

Begin to discover what inspires you, what motivates you and what gets you excited in life and invest in yourself, personal development for growth in the areas of self-growth, financial growth and spiritual growth. Create a game plan for what you want to do to impact others. Surround yourself with people who are doing what you want to be doing. If there is nobody doing what you're wanting to do surround yourself with people who will support you in your vision and take massive, intentional action and don't stop until you achieve your goals.

So who will you be? Will you be a Lane Changer or will you forever be stuck in the trucks only lane looking for shortcuts on an overcrowded highway leading nowhere?

This is our time. This is our opportunity. This is our journey. This is our destiny.

Our purpose is to help others get where we know they can go. We have been given prosperity and it's time for us help others prosper too. It's our responsibility to help people lead themselves. I'm not giving people fish, I'm giving them the pole to catch their own. But I will stand beside them while they cast their reel and I'm throwing in my line with you.

You exemplify servant leadership.

It's not about how much we have, it's about how much we have to give.

And time is something we never get back so let's make the most of it. Creating a living legacy will empower others to create their own legacies.

It's time to play a big game. It's time to stop being insignificant and show the world our true significance. People will know you're a Lane Changer not because of what you do but because of who you are. The impact on others will be remembered by millions.

And I can't do this alone. I need you. Together, we can alter the current mediocrity that has become the status quo and turn into a Revolution of true leaders.

Don't let life pass you by. Bypass the good life on the way to your best life. Make a shift and take your life into overdrive. It's time to accelerate your dreams. You are a Lane Changer!

Aldo Vides was born and raised in the greater Los Angeles area, and moved to San Diego in 2007 to pursue his studies in Economics at San Diego State University, where he graduated in 2010. During his senior year, Aldo was President of the Hispanic Business Student Association as well as a founder of the fraternity Beta Gamma Nu.

After college Aldo spent 2 years working in the corporate sector and then in the non-profit sector for another two years. After balancing his jobs and passion for investing in Real Estate for the last two years, Aldo was able to make a lane change and take the leap of faith this year and focus on his Real Estate passion full time. Aldo is currently a partner with Pacific Property Solutions, LLC and owner of AV Property Solutions, LLC.

www.housebuyersd.com

Joe Zanotelli has been an electrical engineer for 25 years, holding 3 US patents. He currently sits as the executive director for a non-profit, "Academics Through Athletics," which focuses on scholarships for underprivileged high school athletes to attend college.

Through his passion for his personal transformation and his love of people, Joe launched a personal coaching program, helping others engineer their lifestyles.

Joe is a father of 2 lovely children, Stephen and Jacy. Joe has his private pilot's license and has been to all 7 continents.

www.JoeZanotelli.com

Savannah-Brooklyn Ross is the President of Rich Mom Enterprises Inc.

With no experience she became the largest individual buyer of Real Estate in the Nation. Her real estate investment program teaches a simple formula to acquiring high equity, high cash flow properties and has led many others to create multi-million dollar empires.

This Woman of the Year award recipient will be the first to tell you that she is not passionate about real estate or wealth. These resources have allowed her to follow her true passion of raising the conscious level of parents, providing them with the tools needed to raise a generation of leaders. Her young entrepreneurs program provides young people with the confidence needed to develop business strategies that emerge from the soul and the tools needed to build success in all areas of their lives.

She is dedicated to empowering others to create their own success stories. Savannah and her family enjoy giving back by building homes and feeding families in third world countries.
www.richmom.com

Darnell G. Davis is the CEO/Founder of Evolve Media Group Inc. as well as a Writer,   Speaker,   Motivator,

Entrepreneur, and Business Success Coach. For nearly a decade he has been in the business of seeing great people do great things. He has traveled around the country motivating and inspiring people to change.

His passion is to empower entrepreneurs and business owners to create substantial success and expand based on their growth potential. He loves to help people understand specifically what it takes to build successful networks and think outside of normal borders with no limits. He has a very successful background in business finance and marketing. In addition Darnell is an innovator with a remarkable ability to determine and dictate success strategy to seize global market opportunities.

www.NetworkwithDarnell.com

Jay and Annie started their real estate career by simply renting out their personal home after purchasing a bigger home for their family in 2004. Several years and countless experiences later, Jay and Annie have built a massive real estate investment business in multiple states. They have passionately mentored multiple people through building real estate portfolios in the millions. They also employ multiple people in the local community to rehab homes their students have purchased.

Based on this enjoyment and their love for life and helping others, Jay and Annie have an ultimate goal of giving back and helping others fulfill their visions of financial freedom. Annie throughly enjoys helping Jay with his business. As a real estate investor/agent, Annie not only provides support and guidance but valuable knowledge about the industry.

The most joy Jay and Annie receive, other than from their 4 children and their personal life together, is from mentoring others through the home investment process. Although they are very passionate about real estate, they are even more so about helping others. They have developed a non profit that helps children with medical needs that are not covered by insurance companies.

www.visionfocusedlife.com

Stacey Ellen is a Life and Business Strategist, CEO of Stacey Ellen Enterprises, and creator of Joy to Success. As a certified transformational coach, speaker, and mentor, Stacey guides her clients to connect with their unlimited power of joy to double sales revenues, accelerate career growth, and flourish through life's biggest transitions. Her inspirational speaking and coaching helps people leverage their joy and learn specific strategies to accomplish their biggest dreams.

With a love for business, Stacey has 14 years of relationship building skills and has helped over 9 companies experience exponential growth. Her coaching style is highly intuitive, motivational, and empowering. Stacey's clients experience greater self-confidence, a deeper knowledge of themselves, and the skills to help create anything in life.

www.StaceyEllen.com

Rob Campbell has a passion for people and teamwork which has contributed to his success in several industries for over 20 years; door-to-door sales and corporate sales, network marketing and real estate finance. Today, Rob has multiple international businesses spanning more than 14 countries and growing.

Specializing in "personal wealth creation" and sound money principles involving precious metals, he shares methods for maximizing savings, building assets, residual income, and "legacy resources". He's presently coaching and mentoring individuals in this area for success in life and business. Rob is also a volunteer, active networker and Internet Marketer. "I love seeing that fire in someone's eyes when they discover one little belief that isn't true anymore and begin a new trajectory. I love traveling in my business and have fun contributing to others success, that's why I'm in the business of life!"

Rob loves to play all types of sports, especially ice hockey. He's also been a coach and when he's not playing or coaching, Rob serves as a USA Ice Hockey official. He grew up one of 6 kids in Minneapolis, MN where he also attended high school and college.

www.RobCampbell.info

Changing Lanes
International

Want to Become a Lane Changer?

Changing Lanes Live is a seminar experience that will help you find success when life shifts. We want you to be a part of the Changing Lanes community so we can impact the world in a greater way. You are a Lane Changer.

Accelerate. Your. Dreams.

Email info@ChangingLanes.com today
and learn how to participate in an
upcoming collaboration.

You can also visit us at:
www.Lane-Changer.com

www.ingramcontent.com/pod-product-compliance
Lightning Source LLC
Chambersburg PA
CBHW070951040426
42443CB00007B/459